AVANTI!

ALSO BY TIM TURNBULL

Stranded in Sub-Atomica (Donut Press, 2005)
Caligula on Ice (Donut Press, 2009)
Silence & Other Stories (Postbox Press, 2016)

Avanti!

POEMS

Tim Turnbull

RED SQUIRREL PRESS

First published in 2018 by Red Squirrel Press
www.redsquirrelpress.com
36 Elphinstone Crescent
Biggar
South Lanarkshire
ML12 6GU

Designed and typeset by Gerry Cambridge
www.gerrycambridge.com

Cover gold: Kindlena / Shutterstock.com

A CIP catalogue record is available from the British Library.

ISBN: 978 1 910437 43 8

Red Squirrel Press is committed to a sustainable future. This book
is printed in the UK by Imprint Digital using Forest Stewardship
Council certified paper.

Contents

Part Two: Mysteries

For Andy Ching

That'll Only Make It Worse

i.m. Francis Alick 'Frankie' Howerd 1917–1992

No. Stop it. Get a grip on yourself, Francis.
We know it's not RADA or the RSC,
darling [purse lips] hardly. No, the brilliance
is *in* the ooing and arring, campery,

cattiness, common as muck i ness
leavened with baritone working claas plum—
ideas above station, dear—and we're blessed;
for are you not belovèd, pallay-di-um

of the national character—it's true—
and repository—as I said to Thing—
of the cardinal comedic virtues:
Shame, Insubordination and Timing.

So, enough with the Grimaldian hangdog:
And now,
                    [lick teeth, compose, smile]

                                                the Prologue.

Part One: *Avanti!*

Show not tell

There is blood everywhere,
sprayed up the walls, soaking
the carpet, the acrid
tang of a recently
docked cigarette, the warm
hum of several million
televisions, birdsong,
radio crackle, no
sirens, *approach with due*
caution, repeat, advise

Labyrinth

I, inveterate chain-rattler, walk/
walks corridors and passages,
threadbare carpet, trade emulsion
in and out the dream swarm attics,
boot heels thump in musty stairwells,
brick backyards and alleys, ginnels,
and duck/ducks under arches, doorways,
entrances with taped-up doorbells,
avoid/avoids the neighbours screaming,
blue-faced landlords, weeping women,
liars, actors, murderers,
the transients and suicides,
into dusty lobbies piled with post
unopened, basement bars and vinyl
cafés, up and down the winding cliff
steps, and last sit/sits on the benches
in the Chinese garden, in the so-called
Chinese garden, shade and shadow,
stagnant pool with sunlight filtered
through the distant buzz of traffic, I.

An Excavation

The grids arranged with lines and pegs, we cut
through turf and topsoil, expose each stratum,
scratching cautiously, guided down by plumbs.
The layers are flecked with human detritus.
They offer up enigmata, half clues
to what is past, bits of leather, glass, pots,
hair and bone, wantonly discarded or lost
by the careless, or carefully laid out.

We hold the fragments to the light, inspect
them from all angles, fill out rough sketches
into portraits of long departed others.
Come night we don't know if we recollect
or invent them; they look like us, these wretches.
Listen now, someone is digging above us.

Death and Art

How now, scribbler. What are you at?
scritch-scratching in your pad like that,
or rattling keys with such éclat,
             such energy,
to bash out some magnificat
             or elegy.

Twitchy, self-absorbed, you're sweating,
chewing your fingernails and fretting,
to set things down before forgetting
             exactly what,
before you started this blood-letting,
             it was you thought.

You scarcely look up from your labours,
to speak to friends, acknowledge neighbours
except, as if gripped by the vapours,
             a nervous glance,
and strain to hear the pipes and tabors
             of the Totentanz.

Yes, Death and Art are what you reckon
all things by, constantly checking
Death by aeons, Art by seconds
             with feverish dread.
One trails behind, the other beckons
             not far ahead,

that's why you try to twine these threads in
to one cord, to stop the panic spreading,
for Art's a sort of featherbedding,
             an aid to sleep,
while Death alone would do your head in,
             could make you weep,

and so, from what seemed a bad start,
creaking in your hell-bound handcart,
accompanied by Death and Art,
          you rumble on
until it all ends with a gnat-fart
          in oblivion.

Now Death and Art's the only book in
town, and no, there's no use looking
down to see what rut you're stuck in:
          It's all you've got.
Art and Death (and maybe Fucking),
          but that's your lot.

Vérité

I am writing this in bed, with
a ballpoint pen, listening
to Jack Hylton and his Orchestra
(digitally remastered) on the
computer in the next room,
next but one if you count the landing.
The dog sighs at the bed end. Pum, pum,
pum, pum goes the tuba through the
Motu 828 firewire interface
and digital powered speakers.
The bedroom walls are gold, the curtains
gold, the drawers austerity veneer.
There are perfume bottles, framed
prints and photographs, laundry,
and every time it rains, it rains
pennies from heaven.

Tay: Autumn

The sluggardly Tay can hardly be bothered,
rolling in umbers: burnt by the far bank,
raw in the shallows. Desultory fish slop
out in the black pools. Fishermen colonise
half of the river, and waders are optional,
the water's so low. There are bales in the
cornfields, potato tops cut and awaiting
an influx of cheap Euro labour to sort them
and stone them and send them to Tesco.
Away in the distance the Cairngorms are
blue, and the stones on the riverbed slick
with green weed. The water's recession
exposes the boulders and channels that
govern the currents. Pebbles in reds and greys
speckle the bank edge. Why aren't you
thinking about words. I am looking out
at things.

An Invitation to the Dance

On railway journeys or in meetings—
deluged by the waves of tedium
that are the strongly-held opinions,
liberally and volubly declaimed,
of strangers; or collegial bleatings,
inscrutable without a medium
or simultaneous translation,
so enigmatic, so arcane

their communicators' systems seem
attuned to different frequencies—
does your reverie increase to trance?
Your body throb and muscles twitch?
Does your every living fibre scream
for jazz-ballet dream sequences?
Kick over the boardroom table; dance
into a carriage aisle from which

the drear quotidian ebbs away
revealing the bright Minellian
hues of the outer spheres: the air
crackles with the startled blare of horns;
a syncopated, wild array
musters, set upon rebellion
against the workaday; and see there,
from out of the aether comes, borne

on zephyrs, sporting wingèd pumps,
the messenger, firm thighed, athletic,
fit as a fiddle, and attended
by fey gangsters who click and jerk
jazz-handed. As he spins and jumps,
submit to this blithe hermetic
prince, and feel your reality blended
into his camp Gesamtkunstwerk.

Bohemians

You notice first a braying noise
and then the public bar's brimful
of quirky hats and canvas shoes,
ultra-skinny jeans and stubble.

Amazed, you rub your eyes and ask,
Who are these angels and where from
and who set them the thankless task
bringing culture where there was none?

This influx fills you heart with hope;
the neighbourhood becomes a scene.
They push artistic envelopes
like it's Zürich 1917.

You talk to them, your life's enriched
with things you never knew it lacked.
They are so nearly cutting edge,
so avant-garde after the fact,

a boundless future fills your mind—
you might be anything you wanted.
One sunny day you wake to find
the rent's gone up and they've absconded.

Oligarch in Speedos

On a mega-yacht, no less, brandishing
an innuendoed Möet overflow,
bronzed, with trouty-pouting babes-a-go-go.
Oh, copper-bellied kleptocratic king,
pray budgie-smugly flaunt your bling-a-ling
to advertise what everybody knows,
you crass comb-over Russo-mafioso,
which is, restraint and taste are not your thing

but, grudgingly, we have to give full marks for
the way you reify consumption, greed,
and keep the grovelling poor down on their knees.
Yes, you're the sort of immigrant we need,
so why not help yourself to half of Berkshire
and annex sodding Knightsbridge, won't you, please.

Jimmy Clitheroe at the Futurist

Stately pleasure domes, arrayed, frontage
to face sea, dens, one will come to realise,
rife with all sorts of sordidity, here at the
end of the line, end of the pier, under
the pier with Pierrot, but one misses McGill's
nuances, aged five. The Clitheroe Kid
is capering, thwarted in his endeavour
to snatch that table cloth from beneath
yon tea-set, and too concentrated are you
with the hooting and hollering as Jim
cartoon careers round the precarious
square of precious tat, authority stand-in
taking lip from squeaky scamp, his
guardianship will be thwarted too, and gasps
go up as diminutive man-boy tugs
and teapot, saucers, cups stay put [for
now—pratfall coming] but what ales
and Babycham are supped and furtive
gropings in the gardens are beyond
your ken for now, little fellow, excited in
the cheap seats. Speaking of cheap, hey,
the Diddymen, what a swizz, Doddy.

Champion

Now what possessed your seven-year-old self
to moon so, for Alexandra Bastedo,
the home-grown, surrogate Bardot of Hove,
like an inchoate Young Werther? Heartfelt
it was, though not expressible as yet,
clipping out the Titbits pictures and, *Oh!*
sigh at each new coiffure, each swimsuit pose;
burn, boy, in anticipation of hells

to be endured, the sweet agonies to come
and Stuart Damon's gorgeous, gorgeous eyes,
perfect hair, suit, pocket square—it's killer,
nearly Perkins, man! Life won't be humdrum
while we've such models. So hurry, time flies:
bring on the love interest, pass the mirror.

Scarecrow

They have brought him indoors again, Scarecrow,
propped him in the armchair, poured him a nip
of Laphroaig (doubles for themselves) and toast
and laud him, fine splendid fellow that he is:

for did he not bring them glories unbekent
in their lifetimes, class and outright victory
at Scarecrow Festival; did not the beer tent
glow all night, song swell through the district

over misted fields and greening woodland.
Hail to thee, O Flay-crake! O Hodmedod!
O Bogle! they cry, glasses in raised hands,
in honour of their straw-stuffed half-a-god,

and Scarecrow tilts his head as if perplexed:
their panegyric's tinctured with derision,
and rough-handling, not kindness or respect,
distinguishes their weekly depositions.

Tonight a boot was left among the furrows;
tomorrow they'll drag him out and nail him
back up again, nursing filthy hangovers,
and leave him to the mercy of the wind.

An Old Acquaintance

Death comes chapping the door at 2 a.m.,
jiggling an own-brand single malt as bait.
So long and anxiously anticipated,
he—half coy maiden, half best bosom friend—
slurs mitigations, invites himself in,
and from the sofa, roiling bletherskate,
holds forth; confides, inveigles and berates;
oscillates between rapture and maudlin.

Through hours of inebriate remembrance,
discourse descends to fractured anecdote,
to he said/they said/something happened once,
and thence to warm and grainy oblivion
until the morning takes you by the throat
and searing, sickening light reveals him gone.

This poem is scratching my arse

This poem is scratching my arse. That's all.
At some point, temporally unspecified,
I will scratch my arse. Maybe tomorrow,
maybe next week, maybe last Tuesday.
Imagine (as you lie awake at night)
perhaps my well manicured finger nails
are scruffling the downy hair on my arse
cheek, gently abrading the soft white flesh
of my arse cheek so that the poem flowers,
blossoms into life and then, as the itch
is soothed, ends. It's quite possible that you
have lived through its enactment, lucky dog,
or are now considering it, past tense,
with melancholic awe. My next poem
will be getting Geoffrey Hill to kiss it.
Consider that a work in progress.

Modernity

We were brung up on Osbaldestone,
sporting Squire of England, whose
career was in delinquency and raced
cricket balls against trains, whose
gilt shards were uncovered, that's proper
shards with proper gilt, booze bottles
tossed in midden, where the tennis court
was soon to be—no oath mind—by Palladian
folly, if you'll pardon my anachrony,
[tales of village razed and shifted wholesale
to next valley] now it's all Darling Harold,
white heat of technological &c,
garages for council houses, what ever
next, scout troop already old hat, not that
they have hats these days, Baden Powell'll
be spinning, and it gets worse, sweat shirts,
how very up to date, how transatlantic,
and think of our combine, Massey Harris,
already laughably museum piece, as will,
one day, the gleaming new Ford 4000
leap off the cover, causing palpitation,
of Vintage Tractor, but us having then
just moved on from binders and stooks,
and now village stacked to rafters,
dormitarily, every vegetable patch and
orchard, ploughed and slabbed. The Squire,
well, what would he say, reaching for his
horsewhip, what would he say?

Ideology

We are playing footy with jumpers
for goalposts, ineptly hoofing a cheap
plastic ball back and forth across rig
and furrow, and all the brutalities
and cruelties are fairly well in place,
though not yet fully developed;
and, yes, one might draw superficial
parallels with the social primates,
but this is an altogether more
sophisticated carry on. Do you think,
for instance, the tribal baboons
of the Serengeti would allow a facility
for clowning or wordplay to ameliorate
the petty savageries heaped upon
the weak? Or can the advantages
of apparent physical prowess be undone
by unfavourable socio-economic
caste status in chimpanzee clans?
Watch for subtle shifts in the group's
mood and dynamic. There will be tears
before bedtime. Goooooooooaaaaal!

House of Wax

Even in motion, even as it happened,
even with the sweat of exertion filming
his torso, he knew—*click*—this stays,
a still in his memory; the flutter
of his raincoat stopped dead in mid-
billow; Tall Paul a hundred yards ahead,
kitchen knife brandished, frozen in the street;
car windows ice-glazed; the street frosted,
February, silent. And later, flicking through
the boxes of bagged cards, memorabilia
filed provisionally with board dividers
by genre, director, title, retrieve this
single faded frame and build back
the colour, action, sound, the warmth
of human intimacy, of conflict, of love.

Room at the Inn

Three Boxing Days in a row, scurrying across the Valley Bridge—
and this long before they put up screens to stop
the seasonal depressive lemming-fest, which they had said
couldn't be done, budgetary constraints, aesthetic considerations
&c., until that bloke went over with his kiddies in his arms,
and then suddenly wasn't the cash found sharp enough—
to open up, because there are barbarians, and thirsty ones at that,
outside the citadel, who have not seen the inside of a bar
these two dozen hours now, and have endured the soft hum
of familial small talk and drunk only in moderation,
and must now be watered like rosetted livestock,
for do they not put bread upon the table of the licensed victualer class,
and will be, even now, battering on the door as sweat drips down
your sleeve, overcoat collar chafes your neck, and yes, for the third
consecutive year, in too-short eighties shorts, comes loping past,
candy-floss hair billowing, the über-creep, the Tories' chum,
James Wilson Vincent Savile; and it's a small thing to hate him for,
we all agree, tapping glasses in fraternal salutation, but it's a start.

Sports Car

This one's got everything: a girl
in a sports car—make unspecified—
doing ninety—though how exactly
this speed's established is unclear—
on busy village thoroughfare,
scraping narrowly between stunned
milkfloat owner, backed-up traffic
and propriety; her—Jackie O hair
flowing, sunglasses a raised visor,
or tiara—zeitgeistean wraith;
this being the Sixties, and mild
indignance wholly à la mode,
chins wag and tongues vibrate for days.

And further, this by winter let
where boy and girl experiment
with cohabitation, though,
not having got, quite, the hang of
being happy in the world, fail,
descend to recriminatory
howling, pan-flinging, and such;
scratch that, mark it up to experience
and move on: life gets better when
it doesn't get worse; and a hundred
yards down the road, is that not the
house of horror wherein that bloke,
the one with the basin cut, who walked
about, said hello, and went to the pub
of an evening, was found with his
brains bashed out by a lump hammer.

Some of these things have the quality
of memory and some are just
construct of rumour and hearsay

and certain sorts of atmosphere,
weather, moss and stone, grief, sunlight,
love, resentment, jealousy, rain,
and birdsong, but all the above
are subsumed to an unbearable
longing to see once, for yourself,
the girl in the blue TR4.

Fetish

'I... expressed the hope that he, in making a limping girl
happy, might himself become happy.'

—Case 46, *Psychopathia Sexualis,* Dr R von Krafft-Ebing

You are a
catastrophic
assemblage,
a random
agglomeration
of tics and
properties,
aggregated
erogenata,
eyes, teeth,
cosmetics
and nostrils,
late cubist
masterpiece
demanding
obeisance,
wild voudou
writhing and
self-abjurance.
Perspective
lost, I submit
to your skull
rattle, blood
drum thumping
ecstasis.

Figurative

Bodies exceed their bounds, rupture or shatter
perspectively, break down to pins and buttons,
then explode again, light flickering from
mirror surfaces. Mud smears and disheveled
sackcloth obliterate limb lines, hide hunched
frames half in shadow. Walk and walk and
walk through the world, absorb it all until
taking, in time, determinate form with teeth
and eye sockets, strong, sinuous torso, legs
and fingers. Objectify first yourself, then
with compass and square, mark relational
lines to the other and the outside, and last
of all, submit to luminosity and disintegrate.

Spleen (IV)

after Charles Baudelaire

Allez! Precisely what the world needs: yet another
ham-fisted English rendering of Baudelaire;
with nouns more or less ordered, most adjectives covered,
and a tone and lexis that's both muscular and spare.

It's a poetastic must-do for the budding Symboliste,
and a quintessential rite of manly passage,
like mooning over Mozzer, wearing makeup, getting piste
on Absinthe-lite, or standing looking tragic on a bridge:

Don't jump! Don't do it! says no fucker whatsoever,
so you slink back to your rooms, smoke roll-ups and scrawl—
with your capsule wardrobe of Oxfam and leather—
and contemplate mortality and listen to The Fall.

You're the latest in a long, long line, Rimbinaud,
who've sought sense-deranged epiphany by way
of opiates, Old Holborn, and dire budget vino,
a noble line of bedsit-dwelling boulevardiers

so make it more version than straight translation job,
and reference your own life and make sure it's stuffed
with irony, ennui, and that it's self-absorbed.
Did I mention irony? (Dear Ed, Is this enough?)

Bright Lights

'Nothing, not even conventional virtue,
is as provincial as conventional vice…'

   —Arthur Symons, *The Symbolist Movement in Literature*, 1899

They come up from the country, these conjoined,
attention-craving rubes, by rattling bus
in best straw boaters, bows and blazers,
welded at breastbone and cheek, keen to make
a mark. Jerking an off-camber tango
the length and breadth of Broadway, they beat their
eccentric trail from agency to agency.
The one howls profanity, while the other
mutters pietistic homilies, but
all doors slam firmly shut. Audiences
granted brought up short, the curt dismissals
cut to the core. 'Don't call us, kids, we'll call…'
Last words are lost behind frosted glass.
They room, bug-chewed, in the Bowery, busk
by day, for pennies. It's part camp meeting,
part burlesque, performed at a frenzied pitch.
The Metropolitans pass by, unimpressed.

Now Then, Now Then

The Corporation's tremulous with nerves:
Who knew there, guys 'n' gals, Sir James of Savile,
their crown jewèl, was a colossal perv.

While Rome groans 'Not again!' on hearing word,
a hundred charidee PRs unravel
and Auntie Beeb is jittery with nerves.

To sell this one's like buffing up a turd:
whichever way you wheedle, spin or cavil
somebody knew he was a monstrous perv.

In Leeds iconoclasts lay on with verve;
his braggart Scarborough stone's reduced to gravel
by family now living on their nerves.

They know when Jim referred to Dolly Birds—
Tarzan yodel, sit on my knee, rattle rattle,
howzabout that then—he meant kids, the perv.

And who green-lit that caravan to serve
the peripatetic nonce's Travel
needs, must be at home, a bag of bloody nerves
now it's out that sainted Jimmy was a perv.

The Two Boidies

As I walked out I saw two birdie chums,
on a telegraph wire flapping their gums.
Quoth one, 'I say, old featherhead,
I'm starving. Where might we get fed?'

and t'other 'Pal, the place to eat's
b'hinuh parking lot where lies the meat
of a two bit hood not missed at all
by his lip, or his capo, or his moll.

The shyster's back to grafting dough,
his headman's found another schmo
to take the heat 'n' his erstwhile frail's
scoped out a rube and trimmed her sails.

S'let's mooch to th'lot and inna darkness
beat out a crazy riddum on his carcass.
You tympanize upon his dome
and I'll play his ribs like a xylophone.

In jook joints an' alleys the cats'll wail
that all is transient, nothing prevails
but from the pool hall to his re-let room
he'll be experienced as a friggin' vacuum.'

Cultural Revolution, The

We are to have a training day, all day,
Monday. The atmosphere sours:
some fuckwit who could not do his own job
will tell us how to do ours.

My Hat

I'm very sensitive, as you'll
    appreciate
when you hear what I've been getting
    up to of late:
I deal only in certitudes,
    never maybes,
and so have made myself this hat
    from dead babies.

I didn't kill the infants They were
    already dead.
I found them, brought them home and in
    the garden shed
set on with spinners, tollikers,
    jacks and gauges
to steam and stretch and stitch the mites.
    It took ages;

but now I have upon my head
    a splendid hat
to shame the baby-killers and,
    much more than that,
to advertise my deeper,
    finer feelings
and my empathy with all God's
    suffering things.

A New World; A Better World

All the hard work, all you've achieved
  doesn't look nearly so thrilling
if you concede that what you've created
  isn't Parnassus, it's Tilling.

Clown Rapture Imminent

See them assemble under tarpaulin,
raggy-arsed, rowdy, dim-wit conventicle,
googling their eyes, goofing and pratfalling,
red-nosed and panstuck, no two identical.

The Jingles and Joeys, Buttons and Beppos
stream, in their thousands, the dusty back roads,
trudging with bindles and holes in their boot toes,
arrive in jalopies which promptly explode;

but nobody's certain why they are here—
on the ramshackle outskirts of showbiz—
none of them has the remotest idea
who ought to feed, what, even, the joke is.

So, on they caper, cavort through the night,
dance by the light of a torched charabanc,
engaging in ever more savage pie-fights
with nail-studded slapsticks and ironwood planks.

They wake where they fell, spent and depleted,
clown-pants beshitten, all covered with flies
as Weary Willy, throwing back his head,
howls 'We are forsaken!' to an empty sky.

Insect Theology

You're a wasp in the living-room window,
smashing your chitinous head on the glass.
Beyond the pane, the meadow glows
where bees and hover-flies flit between flowers,
grasshoppers sing from stems of grass,
the beetles are busy, the sunshine is sweet,
and it's all so achingly, awfully out of reach.

Then the spider up in window-frame
says, 'Man, you been doing that shit for hours:
cease and desist or you'll purée your brain.'
On a chord of silk he commences to strum
a plaintive bass—gnats harmonize on kazoos—
as he wails 'Will we see Elysium?'
and breaks your vespid heart with insect blues.

Revelation

I have selected this epiphanic moment
from the card index. The moor above Zennor;
a tin shaft. The sky is probably bluer
than it was; the moor's just about bleak enough.
The wind, however, is suitably biting.
I make myself alone and toss a pebble
in. Now comes the tricky bit, the legerdemain,
grafting this inadequate metaphor
onto the emotional machinery:
*How can I love you if you will not believe
yourself loved?* The stone clatters into the dark.

Sunlight

catching privet bushes
so that they glow pale gold
between sleety black squalls;
whip up a cadmium
and ochre mix to paste it
onto canvas board and
hold it.

A Date with Elvis

i.m. Erick Lee Purkhiser, 1946–2009

You got a groove going that was catchy as diphtheria
and whipped your acolytes into a froth of hysteria;
you got under their skins like flesh-eating bacteria,
were as sharp as a scalpel and as cool as Siberia.
There were many imitators but all of them inferior;
the Goths could have learnt from you and been a bit cheerier
because you made us laugh but were twenty times eerier.
Like the King of Siam, a Grandee from Iberia,
you swaggered the stage getting wilder and leerier,
but now the world's duller and I feel a bit wearier.
So…
        what's it like in hell, then, Mr Interior?

Your Opponent

He's never lost a bout, nor ever will,
so don't be suckered by his open guard
into going far too early, or too hard.
His slapdash feints and sleights, come-hither smile,
and scuffling gait are double-bluffing guile
implying he's a makeweight mug, a glass-jawed
clown who one good tickle would see floored.
Don't be fooled. He'll lead you by the nose until,

from nowhere, he picks it up, changes stance
and suddenly you're dazed and on the ropes
where—punchy, enervated and assailed
by his unrelenting jab, jab, dance, hook, dance—
you realise, lead-limbed, your only hope
of redemption's to lose well: fight well and fail.

Dejection: An Ode

'He really is a funny, funny fellow.' Stan Laurel

—(in John McCabe, 1976)

It's like
spending
life
chained
to your
own
personal

Stan
Laurel;
the only
hope is
that when
it's just
him left

he will
recall
you as
fondly
as the
first one
did Babe.

Avanti!

It is
a struggle
some days
to set
one foot
in front of
the other.

My, that
is, your,
that is,
our, eyes
fail, her
hair fails,
his lungs

fail, civil
society
fails and
falls. Great
powers
rise, rise
and fall.

Steady,
my friend.
Let's take
this one
step at
a time...
Now!

¡Vamos!

Let's go!

St Martin in the Palace of Pain

How, or when, he came here, he does not recall,
but wakes face down among the samite and brocades,
furs, velvet, diaphanic hangings and silk throws,
the baleful scents of olibanum, musk and myrrh.

He feels the stripes upon his back, still fresh and raw,
crack a little as he moves, and notes there's something
new about them, something unfamiliar, something ...
but can't quite say. Here, it's so unlike the rude cell,

his desert cave, its hot, stale air, the musty stink,
blood-speckled mats of woven rush, his own crude scourge,
the simple leather flail with which he brings himself
nearer to his God. Those welts are old and healed

but these, he apprehends, were dealt by loving hands,
administered with delicacy and boundless care.

Zimbardoland

Poem written on 8th May 2015

So successful
were the trials that
we've recommended
the method be
rolled out nationwide
with immediate effect
adding one refinement
that's a stroke
of HR wizardry
whereby the subjects
in the interests
of efficiency
have been persuaded
to press their own buttons.

Go on. Press it.
You know you want to.

St Augustine's Gyratory

Saint Augustine, bedded down on slate and oat-straw,
spent a restless night, sweated and trembled, assailed
by this vision; a yellow, flying, fire-breathing
devil, which held, in the pit of its sleek belly, a man—

and man and devil were as one. Just as dawn broke,
Augustine started awake, knew the apparition
for what it was   a premonition, sent by God,
of Connery's iconic Bond in Little Nellie.

In the priory smithy, he toiled night and day,
thenceforth, until he'd fashioned, from planks, wrought iron,
string and nails, an autogyro of his own, which craft
he powered, with knotty, oaken thighs, by pedal

over Pisa; swooped and wheeled through clear blue skies,
whistled to the crowds below, and fired off love grenades.

Somewhere Exotic

It's not Provence, Umbria, Tuscany,
or a Hanseatic capital with black
and white brickwork, or Beijing,
or Paris—not even whichever
Rive Gauche arrondissement's hip
and happening at this instant—
not Catalunya, Cathay, the casbah,
Nepal, Malaysia, or Lvov;

it smells ferrous, scented with peat,
and water stagnating in deep ruts;
the air is dusty, cleg-infested,
sweat trickles into your eyebrows
and your brain seethes and pulses,
veins throb and course with love.

Cymag

Surprising how it has seeped into one's
being, all that land; that boggy patch
behind the Dutch barn, not discernible
from the field edge—perhaps with geophyz
or satellite it might show up – which caught
the ploughshares and pulled the Fordson
back on its heels, so that, with differential
lock and independent brakes, we churned
and worked in tacky clay until the plough
came free; and across the field, the wood,
frightening and dark, which had been just that—
a wood—but now's *Picea abies*, Norway spruce,
un-thinned, neglected, spindly, a poor crop,
overlain since with accretions of schooling,
fact, and even—whisper it—the odd opinion;
and beyond the wood the hedgerow where,
one autumn afternoon, we went with tin
and a tarnished dessert spoon lashed
to a bamboo cane, and I filled the bowl
with pink powder, thrust it down the last
unblocked rabbit hole, tipped the poison,
withdrew and sealed it in the earth.

The Great Be Empty

Fighter jets hurl themselves
down the valley then bank
and careen up over the spruce
clad ridge. They thunder above
the wee white house designated
quarry for this exercise; the
wee white wooden house
whence emanate all those
indignant missives to Min.
of Def. regarding flight
path nuisance and think of
the children, I'm at my wits
end; but what jolly japes for
bored or nervy pilots whom
will soon enough be pounding
the stockades and mountain
hideouts of hirsute despots
now grinding teeth, whetting
scimitars and plotting what
new outrage. And the wee
white wooden house rattles
in the turbulent wake and
the smallest girl erupts in
tearful, fearful hysterics,
while out in the meadow
the trefoils, vetches, yarrow,
cranesbill and the national
flouer sway gently in the
afterburner's fading roar.

Nausea

Guns will make us nervous. Butter will only make us sick.
Rerun the Pathé newsreels of ideologues in horn-rimmed specs;

where vicious, half-wit colonels brandish Mausers for effect.
Show acid-addled demagogues in grainy teevee clips,

preaching personal fulfilment and foretelling the apocalypse,
or media mogul robber-barons urging the people to elect

a stiletto-wielding psycho who inspires fear but no respect,
ailing pontiffs, left wing mayors and plutocrats with walking sticks,

and package them and put them on in one extended telethon.
Ensure it's shown around the world, in every bar, in every home,

through cable and by satellite, beamed into everybody's lives
until it's unremarkable, as commonplace as the moon and the sun.

Make us watch it till we're numb. Make us watch it till we groan,
Guns will make us break down crying, butter bring us out in hives.

Meanwhile, None of This is Happening

1. Solar Eclipse, Tottenham

On the High Road, life begins to imitate
illustration: the light gets all Edward
Hopper; the citizens acquire a look
of fifties Ditko and, as mauve shadows
creep across the street, open themselves
to the uncanny, shield eyes, gaze skyward,
anticipating, perhaps, the arrival
of Klaatu and his eight-foot foam-rubber
buddy, or some chimeric confection
with horns, heads, and crowns in abundance.
The traffic is quite silent, and the Palace
Cathedral walls glow rose and white gold
until overtaken by tenebrose
blues and violets and the estate agent,
Michael, steps out to join the lookers-on,
and Tom the Butcher, Dawn and Mrs Carter,
and Ed Next-Door, and Mr Pointy Head,
Ventress and Trixie, and it almost seems
that we're about to be saved, taken up
to the sky by benefic intelligences
come from the furthest reaches of the cosmos;
but there's a chill with nothing infinite
about it, and gradually, as if someone
were de-tuning the contrast and saturation,
colour and focus lose clarity, then
play is pressed, normal service resumes
and folk go, abruptly, about their business;
and it was, anyway, twenty years ago:
more from where you're standing.

2. *Heavy Snow, Meikle Obney*

It is like a temporally aberrant
outlier of the 1960s here,
pungent with spilt diesel and shed cattle,
a wee world in its own continuum,
where heat must be coaxed from damp kindling
and wet slack with congealed paraffin wax
and newspaper sheets; the water runs red
with iron and bubbles up through the kitchen
floor in heavy weather. At night, livestock
break loose and mill senselessly about
the house and cars in approximation
of a disconsolate mob. The hills, grey
and ochre, hunker above us; below,
down the dirt track in Juncus feathered fields,
stands a mire Grimpen in its lethality.
This morning, though, everything is stilled
by a forearm's depth of snow absorbing
all sound. And it reflects and magnifies
the meagre winter sunlight, so that we
are drawn, after breakfast—for no one,
three miles of road below the Witch's Stone
blocked solid, is going anywhere today—
to gambol and frolic with idiot dog
like children, building coal-eyed and -nippled
snow lady, and fighting and cavorting
in a muffled world at once circumscribed
and, seeing out across the white wide valley
beneath the white unbroken sky, boundless.

3. High Winds, Rosemarkie

August, but a trough in the Atlantic
has twined isobars about itself and hurls
hail and squall across the isle and the firth,
rattling us, here in this tin box, as per
the predictions of Mr Socksanshorts,
battle-hardened caravaneer and sage,
dispenser of heavy duty tent pegs,
which, at least, pinion the ripped awning
to the ground while its inflatable frame
flubbers in the tempest. Hard rain hammers
the misted windscreen and dog grumbles
from driver's seat as we resign to playing
house with toy food and tea brewed in alloy
vessels on minimal gas hob. Outside,
where one might expect cyclonic flotsam—
cows, chickens, men in rowing boats, and barns—
cagouled and battered campers strain their way
to overflowing toilet blocks, and tents
and bits of tents cartwheel along pursued
by weeping owners. Each gust of wind
is stronger than the last and we are braced
to spend forever here, enclosed in pressed
steel and safety glass, watch condensation
drops pool and trickle, feel the air thicken
with CO_2. Wrapped in layers of sleeping
bag, we fail to sleep until just before
dawn and then expire, but when the dog
alarm clock agitates and the sliding door
roars back, the world is where it was again
and sunshine offers its reprieve.

Love

In deepest winter, frost on the fence
and on the grass, a clear sky revolves
above us, arcs around us and you
wonder *What must we do?* I say look,
there beyond the stars, beyond the milk-whites,
blues and greys, into the purest blackness.
Out there. It's coming. A lump of rock
and dust and ice, metal ores and minerals;
roaring silently through empty space
towards our little ball of damp and dirt
One day it will be here and when it gets
here, it may be thousands, hundred-thousands
or millions of years, when it arrives
it will destroy this place as if it had not
been at all. *What must we do?* Why, you
must love me; love me as if it were
already in sight, reflecting in your eye.

Happy Times, Old Man

I have cut myself chopping kindling in
the wrong glasses. A flap of skin oozes
crimson; drops spill onto the sycamore
block. The valley is saturated; the Tay
roils, red with iron from sodden moor;
fields erupt with ghost rivers and lakes.
Swans glide where sheep should be.
Everything is upside down. The orchard
is surprised to see itself. Half salmon
repose on flood-banks, hang in trees.
A heron, spoilt for choice, ariel-surveys
the terrain. I carry on splitting billets,
relishing the metallic ping as each stick
cleaves, then rattles as it's tossed into
the ash-stained galvanised bucket.
A steady dribble of blood stains the logs
on the top of the woodpile, last summer's
beech and oak. Specks and spots fall
on cotton sweat pants, on the bark and
sawdust, on the earth. The vegetable
beds await attention. In three or four
weeks, the soil will be turned, enriched
by compost from the bins behind the shed.
With luck the weather will improve and
seeds be sown—kale, cabbage, peas,
beans and beets—before April's out.
Spits of blood dry black on the creamy,
tight-grained face of exposed heartwood
and smear the face of the rusty billhook.
None of this matters, but, more important
by far, is that it doesn't matter that it
doesn't matter: it is time to light the fire.

Part Two: *Mysteries*

Mysteries

Garlanded with vines and flowers,
  comes the golden youth among us,
gliding over the lamp-lit puddles,
        Dionysus, Dionysus,
through the block-work shopping precinct
  Friday night at half eleven;
hear his devotees proclaiming
        Dionysus izzar friend.

From shadow his bright car emerges,
  an Asda trolley drawn by leopards,
and his congregation surges,
  the anxious flock around the shepherd,
decked out, as befits the faithful,
  with L-plates, veils, pink cowboy hats,
in vestments dignified but playful—
  monkey suits and cartoon drag.

Through the streets the band seraphic
  stagger, orgiastic, reckless,
halting passersby and traffic,
  halting blowjobs half in progress—
pugilists outside the Turkish
  stop to see what all fuss is—
pretty soon the simply curious
  turn to honour Bromius.

Hear the clamour escalating
  as the crowd swells all about him.
See the revellers parading,
  pushing, jostling, jeering, shouting
just to see him and be near him.
  Three thousand would-be debauchees
swarm the precinct, hail and cheer him,
  swing from streetlights, hang from trees.

Join the Bacchants, raving, roaring,
  join the wrecked, spaced out and soaring
blissed-up pilgrims who adore him.
  Lose yourself and dance before him
to club classics from Ibiza,
  wave your glo-sticks, blow your whistles,
dodge the piles of twice-born pizza,
  chicken bones and streams of piss,

the tarts and shotters, pause a minute
  as owners of abortion clinics
and pox doctors, applaud, the cynics,
        Dionysus, Dionysus.
Hear the chant as countless swingers
  dressed in latex, lace and leather
call from their suburban windows
        Dionysus izzar friend.

See them all, the squares, the trendy
  wind themselves into a frenzy –
Hermann Nitsch is puce with envy.
        Dionysus, Dionysus.
Plunge right in, forget tomorrow
  drown in booze, defer your sorrows,
fuck the police and fuck Apollo:
        Dionysus izzar friend.

Ode to Joy

On AirWair soles she comes—through Tottenham Hale,
  through Enfield, Edmonton and Hackney Central,
the snows of shattered windscreen glass, a gale
  of indignation, modern yoof gone mental,
the joiners-in who ransack Shopping City,
  hardcore anarcho-somethings flinging rocks
    and bottles, London aflame from east to west,
past burning cars and freshly sprayed graffiti
  unseen by riotèrs or riot cops,
    clutching a tome by Žižek to her breast

She thusly flits, invisible, among us;
  I've sensed her presence many times before.
That day, Trafalgar Square—in the longueurs
  of turgid oratory, some lefty bore
or other's futile braying slowly creased
  the wind from our sails, gently deflated us
    for the trudge home, nothing accomplished—
I felt, almost, impelled to disagree
  with him, scream everything he'd stated was
    just useless verbiage, and yes, I wished

for Action, but more, much more, for Joy.
  In Hyde Park the striking steel-men and miners'
choruses of 'Maggie Thatcher's Bootboys',
  bawled with jocular menace at police lines,
hinted at burlesque. I thought I saw her there,
  in the crowd, roll her eyes and flash a smirk
    at me, and then the decade went to blazes:
Toxteth, Brixton, Poll Tax—dismal affairs,
  with old foes butted-up to work and rework
    ancient quarrels, like a revived dance craze

where cheerless partners retread the same steps,
  decrepit dogs chained on a double leash.
More promising though, what erupted next,
  the CJB marches, Reclaim the Streets,
and Winston Churchill's turf mohican wig,
  a carnival, surely, for the oppressed.
  'Is not the triumph in the taking part?'
I asked. 'At risk of sounding like a prig,'
  she said, 'it's all art school pretentiousness;
    those painted twits are puritans at heart.'

But today, 'These folk have shed their slave-
  morality; when you unwrap it all,'
she says, 'they're simply learning to behave
  like asset-stripping venture capital,
cleaning out JD's and the Sony Centre.
  Now ideology concerns them less
    and joyful acquisitivity's the tops,
they do what they want, not what they're meant to.'
  And dark eyes smold'ring, off she gaily pops
    to stoke the lambent flames of here-we-are-ness.

The Camden Art Redemption Miracle

Serendipitous it was, their meeting,
Nikki and Owen and the well-iffy geezer
who hailed them from the bar, got his feet in

under the table without a by-your-leave,
asked 'em what was the problem, why the frowns,
and over a cold pint they spilled the beans

about their crisis, creative meltdown,
how they were in a rut, completely sunk,
and had to get out, soon, of Camden Town.

First off he suggested some Es or the skunk
he had, by chance, to hand, which they declined,
but he wanted to help and came up trumps:

they were artists of an avant-gardish kind,
he knew, and he knew a fellah who knew a
fellah who'd made this most intriguing find

that they could find a use for, he was sure,
take ten minutes is all, nip to his mate's flat,
a ton fifty, forty, best he could do 'er

for, so off they went to Barclays, came back
and, good to his word, there he was with it,
a pristine print of Disney's *Aristocats*

(1970), release copy, tins a bit
rust flecked but otherwise unblemished.
Cash exchanged, he was off like a whippet,

never to be seen again. They finished
their beers gazing at the five canisters,
a miracle they hadn't even wished.

The next months were all work. They got blisters
using compasses, needles, Stanley knives
and razors on old stock bought in; insisted

their technique must be absolutely right
before they even touched the film itself.
They fell together into bed each night

too exhausted to fuck but overwhelmed
by love and keen for the next day's labours.
Weekends were ignored, holiday plans shelved

as they rigged up clamps, sprockets and frames for
the 35 mil film reels, and at last,
method perfected, cracked the containers.

Spools spilled onto benches and the cineastes'
factory cranked up, working with control
and precision to diligently scratch

on each cat a little catty arsehole,
winding on, with calibrated gears and cogs,
the film to cut, in each frame, another arsehole,

each a close, but not precise, homologue
to the one before; then they painted on
big dicks and dangly balls for all the dogs.

Months drifted uncounted; they thought as one,
tunnelled vision, filtered out all the jabber,
sought sites, commissioned the *sine qua non*

of installation art—a mash-up gabba/
loungecore/bebop/dubstep soundtrack —named
it, the whole project that is (after Abba),

I Believe in Angels, which looped refrain
featured heavily. They found projectors,
made flyers and, one night at the end of May,

had a screening party with top selectors
and trestle bar. The underground elite
swarmed the warehouse, fêted the directors

with their own beer, filled all the bench seats,
packed in wall to wall, sprawled across the floor
though it was cold and dirty and concrete.

Nikki and Owen closed the blackout doors,
prayed in the dark of their damp tabernacle
and rolled. They were enchanted. What they saw

transported them, the little arseholes sparkled,
shimmered and drew, like tiny shooting stars,
the eye around the screen. The feared debacle

had not come to pass, in fact the oohs and ahs
of the art world's cream screamed success. Success,
that slippery fish; so our Dadas

hit the bar hard and went to sleep still dressed.
They dreamed a better world, by far, than this,
where every insight's succinctly expressed,

materials are cheap and to hand, critics
do not cavil they merely deconstruct,
where laymen never, ever take the piss,

where artists are sovereign, usufruct
applies universally to them and theirs,
Ginsters grow on trees and geysers erupt

lager outside swish pavement cafés where
the conversation's always about you.
On waking you'd think they would despair

but no, they broke fast simply and went through
to the studio, cold as a walk-in freezer,
began again the quest for something new.

Epilogue

Solidarity

It's not all Eugène Delacroix, you know,
swanning up the barricades, sporting gun
in hand, chapeau cocked, disordered masses
at your back, swarming toward Elysium.

It's neither a collective swoon in thrall
to the numbing, magniloquent rhetoric
of whichever on-trend demagogue is
presently stowing carpetbag in cart.

It might just, plausibly though, be a hand
on a shoulder, an offer to bear witness
at a board; support in the face of faceless
beadledom, of procedure masking spite;

or only spent shoe-leather; or fortitude
and patience before the gales of windbag
bullies; a gathering up together and
politely, but not mildly, saying no;

grit and the nerve to turn up every week,
or day, notwithstanding weather or disdain;
the will to rally to your friends when asked;
a swig of tea from someone else's flask.

Acknowledgements

Acknowledgements are due to the editors of the following anthologies/ magazines/online journals where a number of the poems included in this collection previously appeared: *Adventures in Form* (Penned in the Margins, 2012), *Best British Poetry* (Salt Publishing, 2013), *Gutter, Magma Poetry, North* (Wyrd Harvest Press, 2017), *Poetry Review, Rising, The Dark Horse, Transnational Literature* and *Twelve: Slanted Poems for Christmas* (Ink Sweat & Tears Press, 2013). 'An Excavation' was commissioned for *The Poem Goes To Prison* (SPL, 2010). 'Happy Times, Old Man' was commended in the Poetry London poetry competition 2014. 'Meanwhile, None of This is Happening' first appeared in the W. S. Graham tribute anthology, *The Caught Habits of Language* (Donut Press, 2018). 'Solidarity' was written at the request of Nadia Drews for a Poetry on the Picket Line fundraising event for striking workers.

Biographical note

Tim Turnbull was born in north Yorkshire in 1960 and lives in rural Perthshire. For a number of years he worked in forestry, before returning to education and then working as a freelance writer. His first collection of poems, *Stranded in Sub-Atomica* (Donut Press, 2005), was shortlisted for the Felix Dennis Prize for Best First Collection in the Forward Poetry Prizes 2006 and he was awarded an Arts Foundation fellowship in the same year. His poem 'Ode on a Grayson Perry Urn', from his second collection *Caligula on Ice and Other Poems* (Donut Press, 2009), was shortlisted for the Forward Prize for Best Single Poem and was subsequently included in *Poems of the Decade* (Forward 2011 & 2015). A selection of his poems was also included in *Identity Parade: New British & Irish Poets* (Bloodaxe Books, 2010). *Avanti!* is his third collection.

A NOTE ON THE TYPE

The text of this book is set in Dante, a classic contemporary
serif which, with its graceful italic, was designed after the
Second World War by Giovanni Mardersteig, based
on medieval types by Francesco Griffo.
It was issued by Monotype in 1957.